Hello, Friend!

Welcome to your happiness and lemonade journal!

You know how sometimes we get those sour lemons from life? Well, it's time to make the most amazing lemonade out of them...and then write about it!

I know, you're probably flipping through me, seeing all the wonderful images and beautiful sayings and wondering, "What am I supposed to do now?"

Well...I have an idea. Why not start jotting down your happy thoughts? I would love to hear all about the things that make you happy. It's not that I don't care about your not so happy thoughts, but I want our relationship to be based on joy. Think about it, if you're having a bad day, you can open me up, read about your good times, and be cheered up! That's awesome, right!?

To get started, here's some examples of things you can write within me:

"Oh my goodness, today I saw a double rainbow and it made me smile!"

"I had the best cup of hot chocolate today because it made me feel so warm and loved."

See, that wasn't so hard, right?

So, what are you waiting for? Start writing!

What a wonderful day!

_____

_____

_____

_____

_____

_____

_____

_____

_____

_____

_____

_____

_____

_____

_____

_____

_____

_____

_____

_____

_____

_____

_____

_____

I am thankful for both the sunshine
and the rain!

_____

_____

_____

_____

_____

_____

_____

_____

_____

_____

_____

_____

_____

_____

_____

_____

_____

_____

_____

_____

_____

_____

_____

Gosh I feel good!

_____

_____

_____

_____

_____

_____

_____

_____

_____

_____

_____

_____

_____

_____

_____

_____

_____

_____

_____

_____

_____

_____

_____

Tell someone to have a beautiful day!

_____

_____

_____

_____

_____

_____

_____

_____

_____

_____

_____

_____

_____

_____

_____

_____

_____

_____

_____

_____

_____

_____

Smiling is good for my facial muscles!

_____

_____

_____

_____

_____

_____

_____

_____

_____

_____

_____

_____

_____

_____

_____

_____

_____

_____

_____

_____

_____

_____

_____

Nobody is going to break my stride!

I'm high vibing!

Yay me!

Unapologetically happy!

This is the real me!

_____

_____

_____

_____

_____

_____

_____

_____

_____

_____

_____

_____

_____

_____

_____

_____

_____

_____

You can throw your lasso, but you can't pull me down!

Shake it off!

Nobody puts me in a corner!

_____

_____

_____

_____

_____

_____

_____

_____

_____

_____

_____

_____

_____

_____

_____

_____

_____

_____

_____

_____

_____

_____

_____

It feels great to laugh!

_____

_____

_____

_____

_____

_____

_____

_____

_____

_____

_____

_____

_____

_____

_____

_____

_____

_____

_____

_____

_____

_____

I have a pep in my step!

Isn't life just wonderful?!

_____

_____

_____

_____

_____

_____

_____

_____

_____

_____

_____

_____

_____

_____

_____

_____

_____

_____

_____

_____

_____

_____

_____

_____

_____

Forever grateful!

_____

_____

_____

_____

_____

_____

_____

_____

_____

_____

_____

_____

_____

_____

_____

_____

_____

_____

_____

_____

_____

_____

_____

_____

www.ingramcontent.com/pod-product-compliance
Lightning Source LLC
Chambersburg PA
CBHW051311120626
46547CB00015B/2183